# THE WORLD'S BEST SOLDIERS

# ELITE FORCES SURVIVAL GUIDE SERIES

**Elite Survival**
Survive in the Desert with the French Foreign Legion
Survive in the Arctic with the Royal Marine Commandos
Survive in the Mountains with the U.S. Rangers and Army
  Mountain Division
Survive in the Jungle with the Special Forces "Green Berets"
Survive in the Wilderness with the Canadian and Australian
  Special Forces
Survive at Sea with the U.S. Navy SEALs
Training to Fight with the Parachute Regiment
The World's Best Soldiers

**Elite Operations and Training**
Escape and Evasion
Surviving Captivity with the U.S. Air Force
Hostage Rescue with the SAS
How to Pass Elite Forces Selection
Learning Mental Endurance with the U.S. Marines

**Special Forces Survival Guidebooks**
Survival Equipment
Navigation and Signaling
Surviving Natural Disasters
Using Ropes and Knots
Survival First Aid
Trapping, Fishing, and Plant Food
Urban Survival Techniques

# THE WORLD'S BEST SOLDIERS

**CHRIS McNAB**

**Introduction by Colonel John T. Carney. Jr., USAF–Ret.**
**President, Special Operations Warrior Foundation**

MASON CREST PUBLISHERS

This edition first published in 2003
by Mason Crest Publishers Inc.
370 Reed Road, Broomall, PA, 19008

Library of Congress Cataloging-in-Publication Data available

ISBN 1-59084-008-9

Editorial and design by
Amber Books Ltd.
Bradley's Close
74–77 White Lion Street
London N1 9PF

**Project Editor** Chris Stone
**Designer** Simon Thompson
**Picture Research** Lisa Wren

Printed and bound in Malaysia

10  9  8  7  6  5  4  3  2  1

**ACKNOWLEDGMENT**
For authenticating this book, the Publishers would like to thank the Public Affairs Offices of the U.S. Special Operations Command, MacDill AFB, FL.; Army Special Operations Command, Fort Bragg, N.C.; Navy Special Warfare Command, Coronado, CA.; and the Air Force Special Operations Command, Hurlbert Field, FL.

**IMPORTANT NOTICE**
The survival techniques and information described in this publication are for use in dire circumstances where the safety of the individual is at risk. Accordingly, the publisher cannot accept any responsibility for any prosecution or proceedings brought or instituted against any person or body as a result of the uses or misuses of the techniques and information within.

**DEDICATION**
This book is dedicated to those who perished in the terrorist attacks of September 11, 2001, and to the Special Forces soldiers who continually serve to defend freedom.

# CONTENTS

# INTRODUCTION

Elite forces are the tip of Freedom's spear. These small, special units are universally the first to engage, whether on reconnaissance missions into denied territory for larger, conventional forces or in direct action, surgical operations, preemptive strikes, retaliatory action, and hostage rescues. They lead the way in today's war on terrorism, the war on drugs, the war on transnational unrest, and in humanitarian operations as well as nation building. When large scale warfare erupts, they offer theater commanders a wide variety of unique, unconventional options.

Most such units are regionally oriented, acclimated to the culture and conversant in the languages of the areas where they operate. Since they deploy to those areas regularly, often for combined training exercises with indigenous forces, these elite units also serve as peacetime "global scouts" and "diplomacy multipliers," a beacon of hope for the democratic aspirations of oppressed peoples all over the globe.

Elite forces are truly "quiet professionals": their actions speak louder than words. They are self-motivated, self-confident, versatile, seasoned, mature individuals who rely on teamwork more than daring-do. Unfortunately, theirs is dangerous work. Since "Desert One"—the 1980 attempt to rescue hostages from the U.S. embassy in Tehran, for instance—American special operations forces have suffered casualties in real world operations at close to fifteen times the rate of U.S. conventional forces. By the very nature of the challenges which face special operations forces, training for these elite units has proven even more hazardous.

Thus it's with special pride that I join you in saluting the brave men and women who volunteer to serve in and support these magnificent units and who face such difficult challenges ahead.

*Colonel John T. Carney, Jr., USAF–Ret.*
*President, Special Operations Warrior Foundation*

**A French Foreign Legionnaire takes part in hostage-rescue training at the Legion's training base on the island of Corsica.**

# ELITE UNITS IN HISTORY

Commanders throughout history have sought to create within their armies special units that could shatter an opponent's troops in battle. However, as the nature of warfare has changed, so has the role of elite forces.

Elite fighting units are not a new idea. Throughout history, armies have contained units that have received superior training, equipment, and experience. Persia's Immortals, Alexander the Great's Companion Cavalry, Renaissance Switzerland's Pikemen, Napoleon's Imperial Guard, and Britain's Guards Regiments are clearly entitled to their elite status. Although separated by thousands of years, they have something in common: they are battle-winning forces. Their very dependability, their willingness to remain steadfast under heavy fire before then launching attacks to punch their way through an enemy's lines, make them an invaluable asset to any commander. Napoleon fully appreciated the potential of his Guard units, often keeping them in reserve until the enemy had been fixed in position and battered by his more expendable line units.

The 19th century, however, saw a change in the makeup of the elite forces. Previously, elites had fought as a regular part of an army on the battlefield. But during the 19th century, they began

**During the Mexican–American War (1846–48) American troops honed the fighting skills they would later use in the Civil War (1861–65).**

to be used more as specialists who could fight in an unconventional way. The British had used bands of skilled woodsmen, such as Rogers' Rangers, to take on the French and native tribes in North America in the mid-18th century. They were later forced to create units of special infantry to deal with enemy sharpshooters in the **American Revolutionary War** (1775–83). In contrast to previous elites, these forces consisted of highly skilled individuals who were allowed to fight independently and to display individual initiative in combat. Similar units, which were equipped with rifles, accompanied the Duke of Wellington's army in the Peninsular Campaign in Spain (1808–14). Yet to many

**European settlers fought Native Americans in five major wars between 1850 and 1900. However, other tribes cooperated, and taught U.S. soldiers valuable elite skills of tracking and fighting.**

European military leaders, these special units seemed an "ungentlemanly" way to conduct war. It was America that took the idea of elite soldiers to the next level. The **American Civil War** (1861–65) saw the emergence of elites that had more in common with Rogers' Rangers than Napoleon's Imperial Guard. The U.S. First Infantry Regiment, better known as Berdan's Sharpshooters, did not fight as regular infantry. Rather, they fought as individuals or in small groups. Their role was to shoot at enemy officers or other important targets. Marksmanship, together with accurate long-range rifled muskets, certainly marked them out as an elite.

The **Confederacy** created a number of "raiding" forces under men such as John Mosby and Nathan Bedford Forrest. These mounted units were lightly equipped and operated away from the main Southern armies. They struck at will against weak points of the North's army and supply routes.

The lessons of the American Civil War took a long time to be learned in Europe. However, wartime experience, particularly for the British, was to cause a big change of mind. The Boer War saw the British outmaneuvered and outshot by mobile Afrikaans farmers. Columns of British and **Commonwealth** infantry and cavalry slogged across the African plains after an elusive enemy. This was an enemy that fought from trenches and used accurate, aimed shots to cut down rank after rank of slow-moving British units as they marched across the open terrain. Losses, particularly in Black Week (when the British lost three battles), forced the British Army to think again about elites.

In response, the British sent what were called Imperial Yeomanry units. These units were made up mostly of men from Australia, New Zealand, and Canada. Mounted on horseback and lightly equipped, their ranks were filled with hardy and skilled frontiersmen who were often the equal of the Boers in marksmanship. The yeomanry chased and harried the Boers as never before and undoubtedly helped in their defeat. This experience was of great importance to the British Army, and they took the lessons learned into World War I (1914–1918).

Yet the idea of individual initiative was still very much discouraged. It was the Imperial German Army in the latter stages of the war, however, that created the first truly elite units (at least in the modern sense). Operation "Michael," the last-ditch attempt to cut through the Allied lines in 1918, saw the large-scale use of

**This group of German stormtroopers in action during World War I are heavily armed with Mauser long-range rifles and hand grenades.**

**A modern-day reenactment of a World War II German machine-gun soldier. The gun is an MG42, a lethal weapon that can fire 1,200 rounds per minute with a range of over 3,280 feet (1,000 m).**

elite soldiers called "Stormtroopers." These units were filled with expertly trained veterans. Stormtroopers went into battle in small units, carrying lots of weapons. Unlike regular units, which were supposed to capture large pieces of enemy ground, their role was to find weaknesses in the enemy line and smash through quickly and ruthlessly. The Stormtroopers would then push deep behind enemy lines to create confusion.

Though Germany did not win World War I, it had learned how useful elite soldiers could be. It used elite soldiers even more in World War II (1939–1945). The defeat of France and her allies in the summer of 1940 was helped along by a handful of special forces. Highly trained bands of paratroopers were used to capture a massive Allied fort in Belgium. Elite German troops seized a railway bridge in Holland by disguising themselves as Dutch military police. Later in the war, German units were be involved in a variety of what are now seen as classic examples of elite force missions. They rescued the Italian dictator Benito Mussolini from his mountaintop prison at Gran Sasso in Italy. They also used English-speaking Brandenburger units to sabotage bridges behind enemy lines in late 1944.

If Germany led the way in the field of elite forces, Britain and the United States were not far behind. In Britain, thanks in part to the enthusiasm of Prime Minister **Winston Churchill**, many large and small units were raised to strike back into occupied Europe. Army and Royal Marine Commandos, paratroopers, and a variety of specialized naval units, launched dozens of raids against the French coastline.

In North Africa, the Special Air Service Regiment (SAS) helped to undermine the German and Italian ability to fight by hitting targets behind the front line. Units raised in the United States, such as the Rangers and paratroopers, went on to play vital roles in the invasions of North Africa, Italy, France, and Germany. They also contributed to victory in the Pacific.

The end of World War II saw many elite forces disbanded. However, they were soon needed again. After World War II, there were many countries within the colonies of Britain, France, and Portugal, that suddenly tried to overthrow their rulers. So in Africa and Asia many small wars occurred. What were required were units schooled in the arts of **guerrilla** warfare, units capable of meeting the enemy on their own terms.

Specialized training was developed in such areas as weapons, survival skills, communications, and medicine. Britain's SAS showed the value of this training during missions in places such as Malaya, Borneo, Aden, and Oman. The U.S. Special Forces were specifically created to cope with **Viet Cong** guerrillas in Vietnam by winning the confidence of local tribesmen and turning them into a fighting force.

More recently, special forces have been faced with a new type of war known as terrorism, the worst cases of which were the attacks on New York and Washington D.C. on September 11, 2001, which claimed many thousands of lives. Elite units such as the Special Air Service, Germany's GSG 9, and France's GIGN have been created to fight these terrorist forces.

**This German GSG-9 soldier is wearing full hostage-rescue gear. This includes rubber-soled boots for extra grip, an abseiling harness, and a Heckler & Koch submachine gun.**

# WHAT RECRUITERS LOOK FOR IN ELITE SOLDIERS

Selection courses for elite units form the toughest military training in the world. Candidates must possess stronger qualities than the average soldier. This is what the recruiting officers look for in a recruit:

• Endurance
Can you keep going even when your body and mind are exhausted?

• Intelligence
Can you solve difficult problems when they arise, even when you are under great stress and pressure?

• Team spirit
Are you willing to put the well-being of the team above your own needs?

• Self-control
Are you able to control your emotions and think clearly when you are under pressure?

• Sense of humor
If you cannot laugh when bad things happen, will you become worried or depressed under stress?

Today's elite forces are taught many different skills. They are taught to carry out raids, to conduct hostage-rescue missions, and, above all, to operate in small groups often behind enemy lines. As the 1991 **Gulf War** demonstrated, these units can have an amazing effect.

In this book, we will look at some of the world's best units. There is not space here to look at them all, so we have picked different units around the world to see why they are the best. They are of very different sizes. The U.S. airborne forces have many thousands of soldiers, whereas the Australian SAS is a small organization. However, each elite unit is among the best of the world's soldiers.

**SAS soldiers in the densely jungled country of Borneo during the 1960s. Today, SAS jungle training takes place in Brunei and consists of a six-week tropical survival and combat course.**

# U.S. AIRBORNE FORCES

The American 82nd and 101st Airborne Divisions are some of the most highly trained and best equipped forces in the world. As the Gulf War in 1991 proved, they are masters of the modern battlefield.

The first man to put forward the idea for U.S. Army parachute forces was General "Billy" Mitchell. He suggested it as early as 1918, but because many other generals were old-fashioned, the idea was quickly dropped. However, Germany and the **Soviet Union** started to develop their own parachute battalions after the war, watched closely by Britain and America. So, in 1939, the U.S. Chief of Infantry suggested the creation of an American parachute formation.

In 1940, the 501st Parachute Infantry Battalion was created. At first, there were not many aircraft and parachutes to go around. But more parachute battalions quickly followed. In 1942, the famous 82nd "All American" and 101st "Screaming Eagles" Airborne Divisions were formed. These large airborne units also had airborne artillery and engineers, as well as infantry regiments that could land by special military gliders.

American paratroops made their first parachute jump into combat in North Africa in November 1942. A few months later, the airborne soldiers made more combat parachute jumps into Sicily and

**U.S. paratroopers prepare to board a Dakota transport aircraft during World War II. The soldier on the left is wearing a reserve parachute.**

**U.S. paras relied totally on good pilots to drop them in the right place. Here is a captain of the Seventh Air Force, U.S. Army Air Force. To protect him from the freezing temperatures at high altitudes, he is wearing a fur-lined jacket, pants, and flying cap.**

southern Italy. By the time Italy surrendered in September 1943, the American and British paras were experienced in this new form of warfare. Yet parachute operations were very dangerous. Missions had to be chosen with care to give the parachutists every opportunity to attack the enemy, while at the same time preventing them from becoming hopelessly cut off and destroyed. Meticulous planning was vital, especially for their next operation, which involved drops of thousands of parachutists in the most important airborne mission of

World War II. By September 1943, the British First Airborne Division and the U.S. 82nd were on their way back to England to join the newly arrived U.S. 101st Airborne Division. Ahead lay Operation "Overlord," the Allied invasion of occupied Europe.

For the **D-Day** operation, the parachutists had the job of going in first to capture vital German positions and hold them until the main forces arrived. The success of the D-Day parachute landings hinged on the various units arriving at the right place at the right time. The first Allied soldiers to parachute behind the Normandy beaches, on the evening of June 5, 1944, were special American teams called "pathfinders." Their job was to clear selected drop zones (**DZs**) of obstacles and set up "Eureka" homing beacons. In the dark, an hour behind the pathfinders, were 822 U.S. aircraft carrying more than 13,000 American paratroops.

Once over occupied territory, the pilots navigated their way across the black landscape using the faint reflections of major roads, bridges, railway lines, and rivers as reference points. Once close to the DZ, electronic receivers in the lead aircraft picked up the radio signals from the many homing beacons. As the lead C–47 aircraft crossed the coast, more than one DZ was already under attack and many

**The "Screaming Eagle" badge of the 101st Airborne Division.**

pathfinders were forced to set up their beacons under often intense enemy fire.

Despite the best efforts of the pathfinders, some aircraft were still forced to drop their soldiers "blind" or on other marked DZs. Within hours, many parachutists of the 82nd and 101st Airborne Divisions had been widely scattered across France. Fifteen hundred men were injured or killed when they came down in trees, hedgerows, rivers, and farm yards. Small groups of lost parachutists banded together to fight their own war. Though the operation was

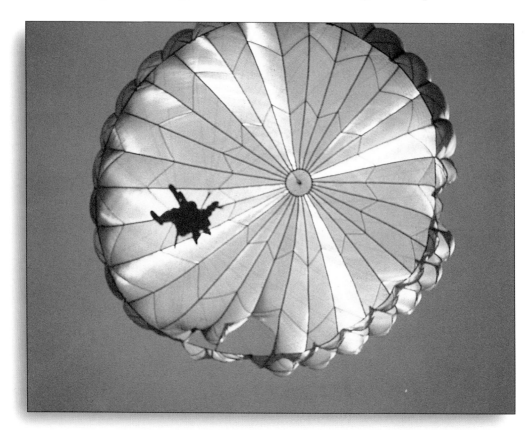

**A para can control his direction of descent by pulling on different ropes that connect him to the canopy. By doing this, he "spills" air from the parachute and has greater control over his direction.**

not going to plan, panic and confusion swept through the German High Command as reports of hundreds of separate battles filtered back from the front.

After D-Day, the two airborne divisions came together again to form a large part of Operation "Market Garden" in September 1944. This was a mission to capture German positions ahead of the Allied advance through occupied Europe. The 82nd Division had a particularly tough job. They had to capture vital bridges over the Waal at Nijmegen in Holland. The paratroops had to cross the fast-flowing river in small canvas boats. Many men died under machine-gun fire in the water. Yet the tough paras still managed to seize the northern ends of the rail and road bridges. A concerted attack on both ends of the bridge by paratroops and British tanks

**A modern para of the 82nd Airborne, heavily armed with an M16A2 rifle and protected by PASGT body armor.**

resulted in very bitter fighting as the Germans fought back from concealed positions among the steel girders on the bridge. Finally, at nightfall, the bridge was taken. The British Second Army's commander, General Miles Dempsey, later saluted the 82nd Airborne, referring to it as the "greatest division in the world today."

The U.S. paras fought with distinction throughout World War II. Only five years after the war ended, they were back in action in the **Korean War**. One parachute operation involved the paras attempting to capture a train full of U.S. prisoners. On October 22, 1950, 1,470 paratroops and 74 tons of equipment were landed astride near the train route. Two days of intense fighting followed as the paras annihilated the North Korean People's Army (KPA) 239th Infantry Regiment and various other smaller units. But as bad weather had delayed the operation, the train unfortunately escaped. However, a few American survivors were rescued from a group of POWs.

From 1965, 101st Division paras were sent to a new war, in Vietnam. Vietnam was not a paratrooper's war, because the country is carpeted in jungle and it is hard to land there. The 101st launched one major airborne operation in 1967, when the paras made a drop as part of Operation "Junction City" in February 1967. The targets were communist bases north of Tay Ninh City. The plan involved a large parachute drop being followed up by a large helicopter assault. The assault went in on the morning of February 22 and continued until mid-May. By that time the Viet Cong (VC) had lost 2,700 dead, large quantities of ammunition, medicines, and supplies, as well as over 800 tons of rice.

The **Vietnam War** saw a change in thinking about military parachute drops. By 1966, the 101st was turning away from parachutes to helicopters. Helicopters were in many cases better than parachutes, because they let troops move rapidly from one area of operations to another. In Vietnam, therefore, the 101st Airborne was designated "Airmobile," which means that they can go into combat entirely in helicopters. In October 1974, the "Screaming Eagles" were officially called the 101st Airborne Division (Air Assault).

The 82nd Airborne Division also served in Vietnam. After the war, they were next used in Operation "Urgent Fury," the U.S.

**The F14 Tomcat fighter flies from aircraft carriers and its wings swing back during flight to enable it to fly at over 1,000 miles per hour (1,600 km/h).**

invasion of **Grenada** to rescue U.S. citizens during a time of political trouble on the island. The 82nd reinforced two Ranger battalions at Point Salines airfield. Then they moved forward to rescue American students at the True Blue Medical and Grand Anse campuses of the

These 82nd Airborne troopers prepare to jump over Kosovo. Once in the air, the large pack over their knees drops beneath them on a long rope. It hits the ground before they do to reduce the weight of landing.

St. George's University Medical School. That these tasks were all accomplished within 48 hours says much for the 82nd Airborne's expertise as soldiers.

The first elements of the division arrived over Point Salines, on the west of the island, at midmorning. They found the eastern end of the runway still held by the enemy. As each aircraft came into land, it attracted heavy fire, and the small runway could handle only one aircraft at a time. After a savage five-hour battle, the Rangers and 82nd Airborne secured the airfield and were finally able to reach the medical school campus by nightfall. Other students were located and evacuated during the following day.

U.S. airborne forces were the first units to be deployed to Saudi Arabia during Operation "Desert Shield." Desert Shield was in response to the invasion of tiny Kuwait by Iraq in August 1990. During the whole of that month, Galaxy and Starlifter aircraft flew the 82nd Airborne Division and all its equipment to Saudi Arabia, Kuwait's neighbor. In September, ships carrying the 101st Airborne Division's equipment and 350 helicopters arrived in the country. Both these divisions were secretly moved west along Iraq's undefended border.

On February 23, 1991, the Allied mission to free Kuwait began. Allied troops leapfrogged by air and land into Iraq. They established large fuel and supply dumps deep inside enemy territory. The helicopters of the 101st Division raced north and quickly seized the important town of Al Nasiriya. The Allies then swung east, destroying the elite Iraqi Republican Guard and other Iraqi units in a series of short battles. Kuwait was liberated by

February 25 and the Americans called a ceasefire on the 27th. Operation "Desert Storm" had been a resounding success, not least because of the efforts of U.S. airborne forces.

Currently, the 82nd Airborne Division is composed of a total of 18,000 soldiers. They are permanently "on call." If they are

## U.S. ELITES

The U.S. boasts many elite forces, and some of the best soldiers in the world. In particular, the U.S. Army has the U.S. Special Forces, otherwise known as the Green Berets, so called because of the green cap worn by all soldiers of the regiment. The Special Forces were created to fight the communist guerrillas in the Vietnam War during the 1960s and '70s, and they became experts in jungle warfare. Since then, they have fought in many conflicts, including the Gulf War, and they have an excellent record of victories. The U.S. Navy has its own elite force—the U.S. Navy SEALs. The word SEAL stands for Sea, Air, and Land. It means that the SEALs will fight in any environment. Training for the SEALs is incredibly hard and few make the grade—about 80 percent fail. Those that do, become members of a very elite force, one which is particularly specialized in underwater and amphibious operations. Together the Special Forces and SEALs form a powerful military force for the U.S. to call on in times of war and peace.

**Paras wait by the runway during operations on Grenada. In the background is a C–130 Hercules, which is one of the world's most important transport aircraft and used by paras around the world.**

ordered to fly to any country around the world, they can be there in a matter of days. As a matter of pride, almost all the division's troops are parachute trained and wear the maroon beret and "Airborne" shoulder tab, as well as the very distinctive "All American" shoulder flash.

# THE ISRAELI PARACHUTE CORPS

Israel's airborne troops have been involved in some of the most savage battles since World War II. Though many Israeli units are expert, the Israeli paras have proved themselves to be an elite of world-class standard.

The Israeli Parachute Corps can claim to be descended from a handful of brave Jewish fighters who parachuted into occupied Europe in 1945 during World War II. Jews were being horribly persecuted and murdered by the Germans during what is today called the "**Holocaust.**" A special group of Romanian and Hungarian Jews were recruited to establish a secret escape route for Jews and also for British pilots shot down over German territory. Many of these intrepid units were captured and either shot or sent to prison camps. One man, Yoel Palgi, escaped from the train taking him to a concentration camp. He made his way back to **Palestine**. Three years later, he was given the task of forming the Israeli Parachute Corps.

By 1948, war in Palestine had become increasingly likely. The Jews in the Middle East were arguing with their Arab neighbors over the creation of a Jewish homeland on the same territory as Palestine. The British were at that time occupying Palestine. But on May 14,

**During the 1960s, most parachute forces around the world switched to using helicopters rather than parachutes.**

**Israeli paras are experienced in urban combat since they have spent a great amount of time fighting in the cities of the Middle East.**

1948, they withdrew and President David Ben-Gurion duly proclaimed the State of Israel. Fighting broke out immediately. As the fighting intensified, Ben-Gurion created the first parachute unit on May 26 as part of his vision of a range of elite units that would defend Israel.

Equipped with only a single Curtiss C–46 Commando aircraft, a small supply of parachutes, and the old RAF base at Ramat David, Major Palgi was expected to produce a company of fully trained paratroops. A core of Palgi's 100-odd recruits consisted of Pal'mach fighters (a guerrilla-type force established in World War II by the British and the Jews to operate behind German lines if the latter's army ever invaded Palestine). However, because Jews from all over the world had come to Israel, recruits were supplemented by a mixture of French Foreign Legionnaires, American paras, and concentration camp victims. The new unit spoke more than a dozen languages and they had little new equipment or aircraft. Yet while Israel fought for its independence, the paras trained themselves into a tough unit ready for the battles of the future.

By the end of the 1940s, Israel had defeated the Arab armies. Yet the Palestinian Arabs fought on with a guerrilla war. So the paratroops were expanded and turned into an elite force. For the next 20 years, they were to fight bravely in many operations against their Arab enemies. They launched daring raids deep behind enemy lines, taking the enemy by surprise and inflicting heavy losses on them. One of the biggest operations was in 1967 during a conflict called the Six Day War. During this war, Israel launched a massive attack on its Arab neighbors. The paras were involved in some terrible battles and suffered many casualties. However, they came out of the conflict even more respected by the military forces of the world.

However, one of the biggest para battles occurred in 1973. During that year, Syria and Egypt launched an offensive against Israel on October 6 (the beginning of the Yom Kippur War). In response, the paras were quickly flown to the battlefield to block Egyptian tanks. One brigade found itself holding the Mitla and Jiddi Passes, while another brigade was fighting on a mountain called Mount Hermo, on the Syrian border.

The paras holding the Passes were fighting a daring battle. They launched an attack across the Suez Canal on October 16. The paras crossed the canal in rubber boats under storms of bullets and shells. Once they had crossed, they had to dig in and wait for the main forces on the other side of the canal to get to them. However, by now the Egyptian troops had blocked all the approach roads to the Canal. The situation was looking dangerous for the paras. But their fellow paras of the 202nd Brigade were coming to the rescue.

The 202nd Brigade attacked an Egyptian base that was helping the attack on the paras at the canal. It was a horrifying battle for the paras. First artillery and then tank and heavy machine-gun fire were used against the paras. A survivor later reported that the shells hurtled in as fast as machine-gun fire. Eventually, paratroops and Israeli tanks pushed through to the canal. At the canal, artillery strikes were followed by air attacks, helicopter assaults, and finally

**A soldier of the Israeli 202nd Parachute Brigade heads out on a patrol. He is wearing heavy body armor under his clothes and his M16 rifle is fitted with an M203 40mm grenade launcher beneath the barrel.**

raids by Egyptian commandos, who fought the paras in savage battles. Nevertheless, the war ended with the Israelis still holding on to their little corner of the African continent.

However, just days before the battle at the canal ended, one vital position still remained to be recaptured—Mount Hermon. During the Six Day War, Israeli troops had built a radar station and fort on the lower slopes of the mountain. Yet Syria now held the summit, and it attacked the radar station with its own elite paras. The Israeli defenders held out all afternoon. Just as the sun was setting, a group of Syrian commandos finally scaled the walls with ropes and grappling hooks and poured into the underground chambers to end the siege.

The fort remained in Syrian hands, even though Israeli infantry threw themselves hard into a counter-attack. With the time of the cease-fire approaching, the radar station looked likely to remain

**Wearing typical patrol gear, this para carries IMI rifle grenades in his backpack.**

under Arab control. On October 21, the Israelis launched a last-ditch counterattack, landing a paratroop brigade on the summit of the mountain, while infantry stormed the fort positions from below. The Arab commandos fought back valiantly, knocking out most of the Israeli tanks. Despite being trapped between the paras and the infantry, the Syrians held out throughout the night. Finally, at 10 A.M. the next morning and a short time before the cease-fire was due to happen, the Israeli paras and infantry threw themselves into the attack, and overwhelmed the defenders.

The war in 1973 caught the Israelis by surprise. It forced them to rethink their tactics. There was another type of elite unit in Israel connected with the Parachute Corps. These were the "Sayeret" units, formed to conduct long-range patrols and undercover operations along Israel's borders and behind enemy lines. There were various and different Sayeret groups. One of them, "Sayeret Mat'kal," is still among the world's most elite counterterrorist units.

Israel's most daring international operation using a Sayeret unit was the rescue of the passengers from an Air France airliner in 1976. The Airbus aircraft was hijacked by terrorists on June 27 and flown to Entebbe airport, Uganda, Africa. Once on the ground, the hostages were guarded by terrorists and Ugandan soldiers—rescue seemed impossible. In the early hours of July 4, four aircraft landed at Entebbe carrying a Sayeret Mat'kal hostage-rescue unit, some Israeli paras, and the elite Golani infantry brigades. In an incredible operation, the Sayeret Mat'kal soldiers rescued all the hostages, killing 13 terrorists at the cost of only one

Paras take on the enemy in a vicious street battle. This scene shows why paras have to be incredibly fit—the running soldier is carrying a machine gun that weighs over 22 pounds (10 kg).

**Deserts can be very windy places, so the para must gather his parachute in as quickly as possible when he lands.**

man. While they were doing this, the infantry and paras blocked Ugandan soldiers from helping the terrorists. The entire operation was completed in 53 minutes.

Israeli paratroops are among the world's best soldiers. Because the Middle East has had so many problems, the paratroops regularly find themselves fighting. This means that their skills have to be kept sharp all the time. Paratroops wear the standard Israeli uniform with a maroon beret and silver parachute wings on the left breast.

# PARACHUTES IN WAR

The Soviet Union and Italy were the first countries to think of using soldiers dropped by parachute to fight in wars. However, it was the Germans in World War II who brought the idea to life. Just before the start of World War II, they trained elite parachute battalions. These were used brilliantly when Germany invaded Belgium and Holland in 1940. German paratroops even captured the whole island of Crete after a series of daring parachute jumps, though they lost huge numbers of men. The success of these operations convinced the British Prime Minister Winston Churchill that the Allies should have their own parachute troops. Immediately, he called for the creation of a 5,000-man parachute unit. Both the British and the U.S. soon had large units. They even started dropping jeeps and guns by parachute. All sides used paratroopers heavily during the war, but parachute missions resulted in many deaths among the soldiers. After the war, parachutes were rarely used again in battle. Instead, airborne soldiers preferred to be taken into battle by helicopters or aircraft. Yet elite units are still trained in special parachute techniques—such as night-parachuting. Parachuting remains one of the most secretive ways to infiltrate the enemy's defenses and the world's elites will continue to keep parachute jumping alive.

# SPETSNAZ

Highly secretive and deadly, Spetsnaz units were not even acknowledged to exist by the Soviet Union for very many years. These crack troops are trained to do a wide variety of special mission including assassination, sabotage, and disabling enemy nuclear weapons.

The Spetsnaz are the elite soldiers of Russia and the former Soviet Union. They receive training in many different types of elite operation. These include: intelligence gathering, long-range **reconnaissance** patrols, taking hostages, attacking abroad, supporting guerrilla fighters, sabotage, and assassinations.

The first recorded use of special forces by the Soviets occurred soon after the **Russian Revolution**. Small elite units were created to subdue those who did not want the communist regime. They did this with such success that more elite units were created. The Soviets also pioneered the use of airborne special forces. Reconnaissance teams, formed in 1927, were used against Afghan insurgents in 1929 and in Central Asia. By 1932, the regular airborne forces had become almost completely dedicated to deep reconnaissance and to the destruction of the enemy's command and control facilities.

By the early 1930s, Soviet special operations units had largely crushed the majority of domestic dissent and felt ready to

**Spetsnaz soldiers during a training exercise. Although elite, Spetsnaz form part of quite a large unit—of around 29,000 troops.**

**All Spetsnaz troops are martial arts experts. Unarmed combat represents an integral part of their training.**

concentrate on directing their attention against anti-Soviet activity abroad. In 1936, the government created an Administration for Special Tasks to implement the ruthless elimination of its enemies abroad. During the Spanish Civil War (1936–39), for example, the newly formed People's Commissariat of Internal Affairs—now the KGB—and the Main Intelligence Directorate of the General Staff undertook terrorist, sabotage, and guerrilla activities behind Nationalist lines on a scale never before envisaged.

Yet it was World War II that saw the creation of many of the Soviet elite forces. They played a crucial part in the ultimate Soviet victory and fought in some of the most hostile environments imaginable—above the arctic circle in northern Russia, Finland, and Norway, and in the Soviet Far East. Special navy units were also created. These undertook aggressive search and destroy missions against German positions on the coast and did daring operations to snatch prisoners.

Most elite troops at this time were selected on the basis of their absolute loyalty to the Communist Party, and also their toughness and stamina. Most were between 18 and 30 years old and, in many cases, were very experienced sportsmen and hunters. Training was incredibly tough. Even in training exercises, injured and exhausted soldiers

**This Spetsnaz soldier strikes a fearsome pose. He is armed with a bayonet, which slots into the end of his AK74 assault rifle.**

were simply left on their own without help. The same happened on real missions and meant that the special forces suffered a very high casualty rate.

Yet they conducted some of the most daring raids of the war. During the winter of 1942–43 alone, Special Forces groups behind the lines derailed 576 trains and five armored trains, blew up about 300 tanks, 650 other vehicles, and more than 300 rail and road bridges, killing and wounding thousands of enemy soldiers in the process.

Two particular missions stand out. In July 1943, 316 Spetsnaz were parachuted into action up to 186 miles (300 km) behind the Germans' front line. With help from local people, they laid more than 3,500 explosive charges on over 435 miles (700 km) of railway track and blew the track sky high. This mission made travel around the vast distances of Russia very difficult for the Germans. It also had the effect of making the Germans very nervous, even when they were in places that were previously thought safe.

The other mission occurred on the night of March 11, 1943. A 23-man party of Spetsnaz led by Lieutenant I.P. Kovalev parachuted behind German lines in the Novorzhev area. After making contact with partisans, the Spetsnaz went into action on March 17. Silently and stealthily, they set about laying explosive charges on local roads and railway lines. They often worked under the very noses of German sentries. Such men must have had nerves of steel. Over the next seven months, the group sabotaged one mile (1.6 km) of telephone lines, two and a half miles (4 km) of railway track, and 17 bridges. These actions resulted in the destruction of two tanks, eight truck-loads of ammunition, several dozen vehicles, and 16 military trains. When the partisans and commandos linked up with the Red Army in October 1943, Kovalev was awarded a medal called the Hero of the Soviet Union, with the rest of the party receiving the Order of the Patriotic War or Red Star.

After World War II, Spetsnaz forces were used in many different operations, particularly in suppressing people who did not want to be under communist control. Yet one of their biggest operations was when the Soviet Union invaded and occupied the country of Afghanistan in 1979. Between December 8 and December 10, 1979, some 14 days before the invasion, Spetsnaz troops moved in to capture a vital tunnel that would be used by the main Soviet

**Spetsnaz soldiers perform a fighting exercise. Though they wear normal Russian army uniforms, Spetsnaz troops are often distinguished by a blue and white striped T-shirt worn beneath their jackets.**

**Mujahedeen guerrillas were feared by all Russian soldiers in Afghanistan.**

invasion. Then the Spetsnaz captured Kabul International Airport (Kabul is the capital of Afghanistan). Over the next few days, the Spetsnaz soldiers accomplished many missions before the main invasion force arrived and took over Afghanistan in a matter of days.

But the occupation was not to be a quiet one. Afghan guerrillas—called the Mujahedeen—fought hard over the next nine years to throw the Soviet troops out of their country. That is why, in 1983, Spetsnaz forces again went on the offensive. Working from heavily armored helicopters, they attacked isolated towns and villages, which the Mujahedeen had once considered safe. Villages suspected of helping the guerrillas were burned to the ground in vicious operations. Some of these operations may have even been carried out by Spetsnaz disguised as guerrillas.

In the spring of 1985, Spetsnaz troops began to fight with conventional units in an attempt to rid the Afghan valleys of the enemy. Helicopters would fly the Spetsnaz troops over the mountains in front of the advancing tanks to catch the unsuspecting enemy in the open. Casualties on both sides were heavy, though the Soviets appeared willing to pay this high price.

But the Spetsnaz soldiers became known as some of the toughest in the world. These troops were battle-hardened and excellent at mountain warfare. They quickly began to notch up successes. Reconnaissance units operated from camouflaged hides high in the mountains. Some groups were disguised as Afghan people so that they could move freely about the mountain passes. Others were dropped many miles from their targets, traveling through the night to lay ambushes and observe the Mujahedeen. The role of Spetsnaz within Afghanistan was vital. However, the constant death toll among Soviet troops in Afghanistan made the war very unpopular

**A soldier is thrown by an expert side-kick during a counterterrorist exercise. The Spetsnaz troops wear white helmets so that they stand out and are not shot by mistake in the confusion of the exercise.**

# THE COLD WAR

The Cold War (1945–1989) was not really a war at all. It actually describes the hostility between the Soviet Union and the Western powers (United States, Britain, and much of Europe) which nearly, but not quite, resulted in war. The Cold War began at the end of World War II, when Germany had been conquered by the Soviet Union from the east and Allied forces from the west. The Soviet Union held onto many of the countries it had passed through during the conflict and made them communist, an idea to which the West was opposed. Germany was cut in half and eventually a huge wall was built through Berlin (separating East and West Germany), with the communists on one side and the Western powers on the other. The Cold War lasted for over 40 years. Both sides felt the others' view of life was dangerous. Both had nuclear weapons and made it clear that they would use them if the other side attacked. Though many wars between communism and democracy happened around the world, the two superpowers of the United States and the Soviet Union never fought each other, though they came close on several occasions. Eventually, the Cold War ended when the old communist regime in Russia collapsed in 1989. The Berlin Wall, the last bastion of Cold War politics, was torn down and there began a new era in world history.

back at home. In 1989, all Soviet forces withdrew from the country.

The Special Operations Brigade is the basic Spetsnaz unit. Each brigade usually includes three or four parachute battalions. A Spetsnaz brigade has between 1,000 and 1,300 men. It is trained to operate either as a single unit or as many smaller units.

Russia is very different today. In 1989, the forces of **communism** in Russia collapsed. Russia's old enemies in the West—particularly the United States and Great Britain—became Russia's friends. Before this happened, much of the Spetsnaz training was concerned with what to do in case of a war against the United States and her allies. Now they train for different wars.

**A Spetsnaz soldier dressed in full camouflage and armed with an AK74 rifle.**

One of their biggest uses today is fighting the terrible crime wave that is sweeping across Russia. The war against crime is a hard one, because the criminals are often organized into huge gangs with lots of dangerous weapons. So it seems the elite skills of the Spetsnaz will be needed for many more years to come.

# THE BRITISH SAS

**The Special Air Service is the most highly trained special forces unit in the world. Since it was created in World War II, the Regiment has achieved some startling victories. Today, it is at the forefront of the fight against international terrorism.**

The background to the Special Air Service (SAS) Regiment's creation was the bitter struggle in North Africa during World War II. Throughout 1941, elite German forces were pushing back the **Allies**. A way had to be found to strike back at the Germans, especially the weak areas behind their lines. The founder of the SAS was a British officer, David Stirling. Stirling devised a plan to parachute small teams behind enemy lines. He thought that once they were there, they could attack German petrol dumps and airfields, both things which the Germans needed to fight the war.

Stirling's idea was given the green light to go ahead. Thus he created the Special Air Service, at first only about 64-men strong. Unfortunately, the first operation was a disaster. On the night of November 18, 1941, five aircraft carrying the SAS soldiers took off on a parachute mission against some German airfields. However, they soon ran into gale force winds and heavy rain. Two aircraft were lost and the parachutists widely scattered. No targets were attacked and, two days later, only 22 tired and hungry men struggled back to safety.

**SAS soldiers during Continuation Training in Brunei. The soldier kneeling at the front is armed with a LAW antitank rocket.**

The "Killing House" at SAS HQ in Hereford, England, in which SAS soldiers practice hostage-rescue techniques. The walls have a rubber coating, which absorbs the thousands of bullets fired every year.

Undaunted, Stirling realized that parachutes were the best way to attack. So he turned to using heavily armed Jeeps to drive to the targets. In this way, the SAS raided four airfields. This time they had great success. Stirling's men destroyed 61 aircraft and a number of vehicles. Once the SAS had learned the art of desert survival, they went on many more raids.

Though Stirling was eventually captured by the Germans, he had created one of the world's best units at the time. They went on to fight with amazing bravery throughout the rest of the war. While fighting in German-occupied Europe, one SAS unit alone destroyed 70 vehicles, killed 220 enemy troops, and derailed six trains. Other units became legendary. On August 22, 1944, Captain Derrick Harrison and a small SAS unit drove their jeeps into a French town. Unexpectedly, they were met by a large force of German soldiers, many more than were in the SAS party. Yet in the following battle over 60 Germans were killed.

Though they served with incredible results through World War II, the SAS was disbanded when the war ended. Yet it was not long before they were needed again, this time to fight an unusual war. Malaya was a country in the Far East that was a British **colony**. In 1948, Malayan

**The famous SAS badge—a winged dagger and the motto "Who Dares Wins."**

guerrillas launched a war of liberation against the British. Faced with a difficult and dangerous situation, one British officer decided that an elite unit was needed to take the war into the guerrilla sanctuary areas. That officer was "Mad" Mike Calvert, an experienced former SAS soldier from World War II. The unit he formed became the new SAS.

Some of the SAS work in Malaya involved operations in both the mountains and the jungle. The SAS approach relied on the use of four-man long-range reconnaissance patrols. They also made many friends among the local civilians. By doing so, they helped people to

**An SAS soldier, on operations in the jungles of Borneo in 1965, uses radio equipment to communicate with soldiers in another patrol.**

support the British rather than the guerrillas. Infiltrating guerrilla-controlled areas by parachuting into the jungle, patrols gradually built up a picture of enemy activity from well-used tracks, fields laid to rice, arms dumps, and camps. This information was then later used to lay ambushes and launch search-and-destroy operations. A number of terrorist leaders were followed back to their hide-outs and killed or captured by the SAS.

Malaya was only the first of many operations for the new SAS. Next stop was Borneo. This time the enemy was not guerrillas but regular soldiers, often Indonesian paratroops and Marines. The parties of soldiers crossing the long border of mountainous jungle were engaged in sabotage or terrorist missions. Two- and four-man SAS surveillance posts were established all the way down the border to report on enemy movements. This was helped by winning the hearts and minds of the jungle tribes and then using them to gather important information as well. The SAS also embarked on highly secret operations to identify and attack enemy bases just inside Indonesian territory. SAS activities helped to win a victory for the British in Borneo. Indonesia decided that it was losing too many men to this elite force. Commonwealth forces killed more than 2,000 Indonesians at a cost of 115 servicemen killed and around twice that number wounded. The SAS lost only three men killed and two wounded.

At the beginning of the 1970s, the SAS returned to a country in the Middle East called Oman. They had been there in the 1950s, and had amazing success. Now they were faced with a large-scale guerrilla war. This was caused by a group called the People's Front

**This elite soldier is wearing thermal imaging goggles—which enable him to see in the dark—and is carrying a silenced pistol with a laser-sighting device beneath the barrel.**

for the Liberation of the Occupied Arabian Gulf (PFLOAG). It was attempting to overthrow the government of the **Sultan** of Oman and Britain sent forces to help the government resist. The SAS set about creating small military units made up of the local people.

By 1974, the Sultan's 15,000-strong army was made bigger by about around 1,600 of these civilian soldiers, who were led by 50 to 100 SAS soldiers. As in earlier conflicts, the SAS showed that they were real experts. In one battle at a place called Mirbat, a handful of SAS soldiers held off 250 guerrillas. Nowhere was safe for the guerrillas. The successful Omani campaign cost the lives of only 12 SAS soldiers.

Between 1968 and 1974, terrorism became a new problem all over the world. This provided a new role for the SAS as a counterterrorist force. Shortly after, a Counter Revolutionary Warfare Wing was set up at Hereford—the SAS headquarters in England—to provide training in the techniques of counterterrorism. Also Special Projects Teams (SPTs) received their training in hostage-rescue techniques.

One of the most prominent areas of SAS operations was Northern Ireland. From the late 1960s, this province of the United Kingdom had been experiencing a violent and ongoing war between two different religious

**This SAS trooper in Borneo in 1966 wears standard British Army kit but carries the U.S. M16 rifle as his personal weapon. Its lightweight but powerful cartridge makes it an ideal jungle weapon.**

communities. The British Army and government were also targets of the terrorists. The SAS went to Northern Ireland to fight the terrorists at their own game. One area of the Province that received particular attention was South Armagh, known as "Bandit Country," the heartland of the chief terrorist organization. The main role of the SAS in Northern Ireland was, and still is, gathering information. But they were also used to capture high-ranking

**The SAS Mountain Troops are trained in everything from climbing mountains and skiing to arctic survival and mountain warfare.**

terrorists. The Regiment quickly became feared and loathed by the enemy fighters.

Carrying out operations in Northern Ireland was very complex, a fact illustrated forcibly in May 1976, when two parties of the SAS were arrested by the Southern Ireland police after accidentally crossing the border. There were also problems with SAS surveillance operations. In July 1978, a serious breakdown in communications between the Army and the Royal Ulster Constabulary (RUC) resulted in an SAS surveillance team accidentally killing an innocent 16-year-old schoolboy, when he returned to look at a secret store of arms that he had earlier discovered.

The SAS have always operated in difficult environments, and Northern Ireland was no different. Yet it was terrorists from a different country that brought the Regiment to the attention of people around the world. On Monday May 5, 1980, an SAS team ended a siege at the Iranian embassy in London. The embassy had been taken over by terrorists a few days earlier. Though it was hoped that the siege could be brought to an end peacefully, the terrorists eventually shot dead one of their 26 hostages. It was time for the SAS to go into action.

As the world watched on TV, the black-clad counterterrorist soldiers, amid smoke, explosions, and gunfire, **abseiled** down the sides of the building and entered the embassy to rescue the hostages. For many of those watching, it was the first time they had ever heard of an organization called the Special Air Service. The operation was an incredible success, with almost all the hostages rescued unhurt and all the terrorists either killed or captured. The Regiment has been trapped in the media spotlight ever since.

The **Falklands War,** which began in April 1982, gave the Regiment an opportunity to practice other roles than simply hostage-rescue. The SAS were part of a large British force sent to recapture the Falkland Islands after Argentina invaded and occupied them. Reconnaissance teams, which spent many tense days hidden behind Argentine lines, locating, identifying, and assessing the strength of enemy forces, made a vital contribution to the success of the ground operations. However, the Regiment is more likely to be remembered for the more famous raid on Pebble Island on May 15, when SAS troopers destroyed 11 enemy aircraft in a classic nighttime operation.

During the 1991 Gulf War, SAS teams were inserted deep behind enemy lines inside Iraq and Kuwait to assist Allied operations. Missions included finding important enemy targets such as Iraqi headquarters, Scud surface-to-surface missile launchers, and command bunkers. They further assisted Allied aircraft in destroying these targets by fixing them with special laser beams that controlled aircraft bombs. The beam would bounce off the target into the sky, creating a "tunnel" down which a laser-guided bomb could travel. Other operations involved rescuing and evacuating Allied aircrew who had been shot down.

The SAS is currently part of U.K. Special Forces Group, which also includes the Royal Marines' Special Boat Service (formally Squadron). The SAS is based at Stirling Lines in Hereford and consists of four "Sabre" Squadrons (A, B, D, and G Squadrons) and

**Elite troops in action during a live-fire exercise. Trees, walls, and buildings provide excellent cover for the soldier in these situations.**

Each SAS patrol has a communication specialist called a signaler. He
operates the radio, but can also control artillery and air strikes,
make and break codes, and help the soldiers to navigate.

an Army Reserve "Sabre" Squadron (R Squadron). Each squadron is divided into four troops: Mountain, Boat, Mobility, and Air Troop—each specializing in different methods of combat and different environments. Each troop consists of four, four-man fighting patrols. In turn, each of these has a signaler, linguist (someone who is good at speaking foreign languages), a medic, and a demolitions specialist. The SAS remains Britain's most specialized unit, and possibly the world's greatest elite force.

## SAS JUNGLE TRAINING

The first thing that SAS instructors do when the new recruits arrive on their jungle survival course is try to get them used to the jungle. For many it comes as a shock. Everything is different: the climate, the trees and plants, and the animals. During their four to six weeks in the jungle, the recruits are taught to find food and water. These things are actually quite easy to do because the jungle is bursting with life. What is difficult is avoiding the many poisonous plants and animals that live there, and also coping with many tropical diseases. Because of this, SAS soldiers are taught how to recognize dangerous wildlife and plant life and avoid it. They are also taught how to treat themselves and friends for illnesses that could be fatal in the jungle. SAS soldiers have used their jungle survival skills in places such as Malaya and Borneo.

# THE AUSTRALIAN SAS REGIMENT

The Australian SAS Regiment, like its British counterpart, is highly trained and superbly equipped. Formed during the 1950s, it saw extensive service in Vietnam, where it achieved much success. The Regiment is now rated by many experts as being among the best in the world.

Today's Australian elite units have their roots in World War II. The Imperial Japanese Army came close to Australia's shores when it invaded New Guinea and the Pacific islands in early 1942. Across a short strip of ocean, the remote outposts of northern Australia prepared to meet the enemy with guerrilla warfare.

The Australians knew that they were experts in fighting and surviving in the arid bush and deserts. So the Second/First North Australia Observer Unit was raised in July 1942 to patrol into remote, unmapped areas of the northern coast and report on enemy movements. In the event of an invasion, the "Nackeroos" were to remain behind to report on the advancing Japanese forces. Across the sea, other groups, such as the civilian Coastwatchers and M Special Force, also collected vital intelligence from behind the lines. Some special groups actually fought the Japanese, such as the Australian Independent Commando Companies and Z Special Force who took the war into the enemy's camp.

**The Australian SAS survived for long periods in enemy territory during the Vietnam War. One of their lifelines was the Chinook helicopter.**

At the end of the war, all but a few regular Australian Army infantry units were demobilized as the danger receded. The move toward a post-war elite airborne unit began on October 23, 1951. On this date an airborne platoon of the Royal Australia Regiment (RAR) was created. This was intended mainly for rescue roles and was also there as a rapid-reaction force in case of national emergencies. Two Commando units were also raised in 1955.

It took until 1957 before the First Australian SAS company was created. The primary role of the new SAS unit was reconnaissance— inserting parachutists deep into enemy territory to gather intelligence. The Company was organized as a commando unit line and was based at Swanbourne Barracks, Perth (northern Australia). The men wore

**Weapons training is important to all special forces. Shown here are weapons typical of a patrol—a U.S. M60 machine gun (at the front) for heavy fire, and FN FAL rifles as personnel weapons.**

red berets with the crossed rifles of the Royal Australian Infantry Corps. They spent the next few years training in the hostile terrain of northwestern Australia. These exercises were not without incident, as Lieutenant-Colonel David Horner tells us: "Two other members of the company had to abandon a 12-foot rubber **dinghy** when a crocodile climbed aboard. Sharks were in the area, but the two men gingerly pulled up the anchor and towed the dingy ashore with the crocodile as a passenger."

The Australian SAS troops were soon fighting in Borneo alongside the British and New Zealand SAS. They proved that they were excellent soldiers, and so the Australian authorities decided to expand them in size. The new unit had a total of 15 officers and 86 other ranks. For a while, the red berets were kept. However, parachute-qualified troopers were entitled to wear the distinctive drooped SAS **Sabre Squadron** wings.

The Australians soon showed that they were worthy of the elite name. In Borneo, they did everything that the British SAS was doing—building support among the local people and conducting dangerous combat and reconnaissance missions into the Bornean jungle. Occasionally, they were asked to lead large forces of conventional infantry back across the border to hit large groups of enemy troops. Despite the increased safety in numbers, these operations often proved to be more dangerous than the reconnaissance patrols. On January 30, 1966, a large squadron-sized force, composed of infantry and various SAS soldiers, was deployed to attack an Indonesian base on the Sekayan River, where it was believed a large enemy force was assembling for a raid across the border.

An Australian SAS soldier during arms-training. Handling a machine gun is not an easy skill. If the soldier fires for too long without pausing, the barrel will get hot and melt.

The SAS squadron crossed the frontier unobserved. They eventually reached the river at dusk on February 3. Intending to catch the Indonesians unaware at dawn the next day, the party crossed the river and advanced along the river bank. Suddenly, the lead troop stumbled into the enemy camp and were immediately pinned down by gunfire. The situation grew worse and worse, and the units had to withdraw. Three SAS soldiers were trapped in a small hut. To cover their withdrawal, one of the SAS soldiers threw a grenade. However, it unfortunately struck an upright beam on the far side of the hut and bounced back to explode among the Australians themselves. All three men were badly wounded.

Suffering severe burns and cut off from the rest of the squadron withdrawing across the river, the plight of the men became even

**An Australian SAS patrol in Vietnam in 1969 uses a U.S. M113 armored personnel carrier to get around.**

more desperate when artillery fire started to rain in. Once across the river, the long journey to the border became a nightmare for the badly injured soldiers. They were forced to crawl along pig trails, compasses in hand, to avoid any Indonesian survivors who might be looking for them. Reaching the border around dawn, the soldiers pressed on, finally reaching safety around mid-morning.

Later in 1966, the Australian SAS found itself involved with a new war in Vietnam. The first SAS operations concentrated on intelligence gathering and hitting small Viet Cong (VC) outposts. Soon the VC struck back in force and there were some major battles between the Australian and Vietnamese communist forces. After battles, four- or five-man SAS patrols searched for parties of VC who had survived. Firefights were common, but the SAS almost always came out on top. In five years, the Australian and New Zealand SAS killed more than 500 enemy for the loss of one man killed by enemy fire and 27 wounded. In captured documents, the communists referred to the

**An Australian SAS soldier training in the Philippines takes aim with the U.S. M16 rifle.**

SAS as the Ma Rung or "jungle ghosts." The enemy put a price on their heads, reputedly $5,000, dead or alive.

The Viet Cong patrol that resulted in the single SAS death provides a fascinating picture of these operations. On January 17, 1967, an SAS patrol, commanded by Sergeant Norm Ferguson, was dropped by helicopter into an enemy-controlled area of open grassland and jungle. Sounds could be heard from a VC base nearby. The next morning, as the patrol began to circle the enemy camp, an ambush was sprung from the patrol's left side. Private Russell Copeman, the patrol's medic, was hit twice by enemy fire. The patrol reacted quickly, and exploded smoke grenades before disappearing back into the jungle.

However, the patrol was now hampered by the badly wounded man. It just managed to just keep ahead of the enemy search parties. Over the next hour, and with the enemy in almost continual contact, the patrol stopped only briefly to dress the medic's wounds and radio for a helicopter rescue. When the **RAAF** helicopter appeared overhead, Copeman and another soldier were lifted aboard. But the enemy charged into the small clearing, despite a constant hail of fire from the helicopter door-gunner. The last man to be extracted was Sergeant Ferguson, who was forced to fire at a party of VC who rushed into the clearing while he was still dangling from the aircraft's winch rope. Sadly, Copeman died four months later from complications due to his injuries.

During Australia's 10-year involvement in Vietnam, the SAS squadrons were usually rotated on nine-month attachments to the main Task Force. Long-range reconnaissance patrols still formed the majority of the Regiment's work. Yet ambushes, raids, and prisoner snatches were also undertaken. Some of the last operations included running patrols into dangerous VC sanctuary areas such as the May Taos Mountains. Other tasks included prisoner of war (POW) rescue operations ("Bright Light" missions) with the U.S. SEALs. The Australians finally left Vietnam in December 1972.

In the aftermath of the Vietnam War, the SAS were given two new roles inside Australia: conducting regional long-range surveillance patrols (LRSPs) in the vast northwestern deserts, and counterterrorism. The final impetus to create an Australian hostage-rescue/counterterrorist (HRU/CT) force was provided by the bombing of the Hilton Hotel in Sydney on February 13, 1978. A year later, permission was given to establish the Tactical Assault

**Australian soldiers prepare to fire at the "enemy" during exercises at Shoalwater Bay Training Facility, in Queensland, May 2001.**

Group (TAG) within SASR to provide specialist support for the Commonwealth Police.

Like other modern elite forces, the Australian SAS are now experts in fighting terrorism and rescuing hostages as well as battles on open ground. There is a special Training Squadron, which is responsible for selection and advanced training. The Australian SAS wears standard Australian Army uniforms with the distinctive sand-colored beret and the famous winged dagger SAS badge.

## THE VIETNAM WAR

The Vietnam War was one of the saddest episodes in recent U.S. history. Vietnam in the early 1960s was divided into two halves. North Vietnam was communist, but South Vietnam was backed by the United States and other anti-communist countries. The North wanted to take over the South and make it communist, and so started a war against it. The United States became involved, and fought there between 1963 and 1973. The U.S. forces fought in tough jungle conditions, and they won almost every major battle they were involved in. Yet the losses started to add up. Over 58,000 U.S. soldiers were killed during the conflict. Eventually the public at home had had enough, and the U.S. started to pull out of Vietnam in 1968. The last U.S. troops left in 1973 and South Vietnam fought on alone. The North launched some massive attacks and the South resisted for two years. Yet in the end it could not keep going, and in 1975 the South fell to the communists.

# WEAPONS AND EQUIPMENT

There may be many different types of elite unit, but they all need to have the best military weapons and equipment available, in order to carry out their high-risk missions. The most important tools of their trade are personal weapons and the transport that takes them into action, and they are the focus of this chapter.

Elite forces throughout the world employ a wide variety of weapons and military equipment, ranging from handguns, submachine guns (SMGs), and automatic rifles, to air-portable vehicles, specialized aircraft, and high-speed assault craft.

Special Forces units undertake a wide range of operations that are notably different to those of conventional infantry forces. The latter are trained to operate on the battlefield as components of a large military machine and are supported by armor, artillery, helicopters, and aircraft. Special Forces, by comparison, often fight as small-sized, unsupported teams deep behind enemy lines. All team members must be highly proficient in the use of their individual weapons, but the weapons themselves, to serve them in their mission, must also fulfill certain criteria:

## Absolute reliability

As special forces missions often involve short, violent contacts with

**Elite forces always have the best kit. These troops carry the All-Purpose Lightweight Individual Load Carrying (ALICE) pack and belt.**

**More than 80 million AK47 rifles have been produced since the inventor—Mikhail Kalashnikov—designed it in 1947.**

the enemy, a reliable weapon is essential. They must work first time, every time. Rifles such as the Soviet AK-47 are crude by Western standards, but a Spetsnaz team using them knows that they can always be relied upon, even when caked in mud or covered in snow. Similarly, SAS hostage-rescue units (HRUs) know that their MP5 series submachine guns (SMGs) will always work first time during a siege-busting operation.

## Weight

As many special forces missions are conducted on foot and over difficult terrain, individual weapons must be as light as possible. Weight is of even more importance to elite airborne troops, who are required to manhandle their equipment into combat. Paradoxically, the trend over the last 60 years has been toward heavier assault rifles—a consequence of the increasing complexity of internal working parts. The .303 Lee Enfield weighed nine pounds (4.1 kg) loaded, compared to nine and a half pounds (4.3 kg) for the 7.62-millimeter L1A1 Self-Loading Rifle (SLR), eight pounds

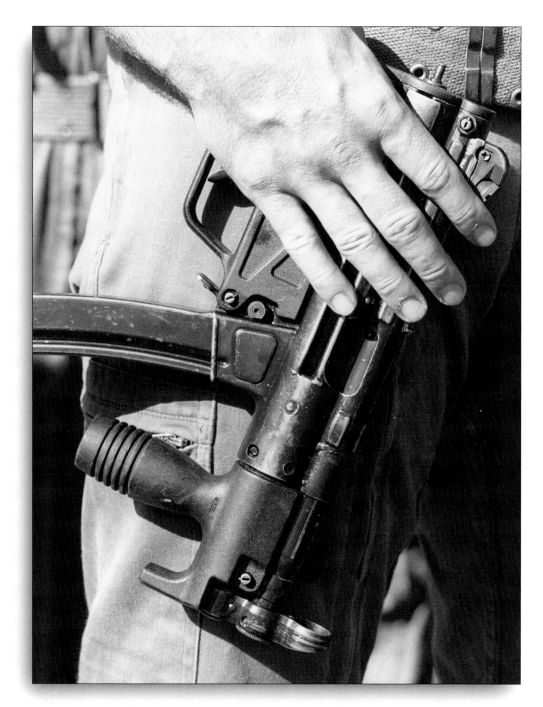

Because elite units often work undercover, they often choose small weapons that can be easily hidden. This MP5K Personal Defense Weapon folds down to less than 14 inches (35 cm).

(3.6 kg) for the Soviet 5.45-millimeter AK-74, and 11 pounds (4.98 kg) for the new British 5.56-millimeter L85A1 (SA-80). The increased use of plastics in the construction of weapons, especially in the Heckler & Koch G11, the SA-80, and the innovative Glock range of handguns, seems set to reverse this trend. Though the overall weight of the infantry rifle has increased since World War II, the change to smaller caliber ammunition means that individual rounds weigh less than their predecessors, enabling more to be carried by individual soldiers.

**A standard British Army pack and rifle. The pack weighs 50 pounds (22 kg) when full, and the rifle weighs eight and a half pounds (3.8 kg).**

## Size

The length of a weapon determines its maneuverability and the ease with which it can be fired from the range of positions (sitting, prone, shoulder, or hip) essential for special forces work. With the exception of the L1A1, later rifles have been shorter than the old Lee Enfield: Lee Enfield (45 in, 113 cm), L1A1 (46 in, 114 cm), M16A2 (38 in, 94 cm), and SA-80 (31 in, 78.5 cm). The MP5K series used by SAS and other HRUs is only 13 inches (32.5 cm) long.

## Maximum firepower

The 1980s witnessed the introduction into service of a number of weapons that had smaller calibers than their predecessors, such as the SA-80 which replaced the SLR, and the AK-74 which replaced the AK-47. The smaller 5.56-millimeter cartridge resulted in an overall reduction in weapon size and recoil.

In addition, the round displayed an increased lethality when compared to the older and heavier 7.62-millimeter bullet, because it "tumbled" rapidly when it hit the target and delivered its energy in a massive fashion rather than passing through the target with minimal energy transfer. This latter problem is especially true of the standard nine-millimeter round, which has a tendency to pass straight through the body of a victim and keep on going. FBI files, for example, contain documented cases where felons were hit with between 30 to 40 nine-millimeter bullets during the course of long firefights and still continued to fight, and even kill several officers, before themselves receiving a mortal wound!

But while the weapons elite soldiers carry in their armory are

**The Enfield L85A1, otherwise known as the SA80 rifle, replaced the Self-Loading Rifle as the British Army's standard weapon in the 1980s.**

vital to the successful completion of missions, without effective transport they will not reach their location in the first place. Transportation to and from a mission has always presented difficulties for commanders throughout history, and this is especially true of special forces and airborne units. Secret methods of going behind enemy lines are essential for units such as the SAS—discovery can mean death or capture. Specialized high-altitude, low-opening (HALO) parachute techniques let soldiers to dropped from heights of about 32,000 feet (10,000 m) and descend silently to their drop zone (DZ) undetected. They open their parachutes only at the last minute before floating a short distance to earth. Similarly, high-altitude, high-opening (HAHO) parachute methods, where the soldiers open their parachutes immediately after leaving the aircraft, are also used by special forces. The HAHO technique lets soldiers "fly" their parachutes up to 50 miles (80 km) before touching down, making it an ideal silent insertion method.

The aircraft used by special forces for parachute drops are also employed by conventional airborne units. Formations such as the British and Israeli paras, as well as the U.S. 82nd Airborne Division, employ so-called static-line parachuting (in which the soldiers' parachutes open automatically as they leave the aircraft) as opposed to **freefall** techniques. The aircraft used include the Lockheed C-130 Hercules. This is a four-engined aircraft with a range of 2,500 miles (4,000 km) and the capacity to carry 64 paratroopers. The giant American C-141 Starlifter can transport 155 paratroopers in its fuselage. Russia, too, has a large airlift capability. It has over 600 Il-76 Candid heavy transport aircraft, each capable of carrying 140 paratroopers.

The helicopter is an ideal, if expensive, tool for special forces operations. No other military vehicle can match its speed and cross-country mobility. There are a number of helicopters that are ideally suited for special forces use. The large CH-47 Chinook transport helicopter can carry 44 troops and was used in 1991 by the U.S. Marines in the Gulf War. It was also used to insert SAS and SEAL teams into Iraq and Kuwait. The American Sikorsky corporation produces a number of helicopter models, which are in service with the U.S. Marines and other American airborne units. Their massive CH-53 Sea Stallion has a range of 1,280 miles (2,076 km). The UH-60 Black Hawk assault and transport helicopter is the workhorse of the 101st Airborne Division. Capable of carrying 11 fully equipped soldiers, it can also be armed with machine guns and Hellfire antitank missiles.

Specialized land vehicles have, since World War II, played an important part in transporting special forces. The SAS patrols in the north African desert demanded rugged vehicles that could carry large quantities of food, water, ammunition, and fuel, as well as people. Today, this tradition is continued with such vehicles as Land Rover's series of long-range reconnaissance vehicles, the French ACMAT VLRA, and the Israeli M-325 Command Car. Vehicles such as the Land Rover are equipped with machine guns,

**The Black Hawk helicopter features a special cargo hook at the side which can carry 8,000 pounds (3,629 kg) of weight. It has an impressive maximum speed of 184 miles per hour (296 km/h).**

**A para of the British Pathfinder Brigade does a freefall High Altitude, Low Opening (HALO) parachute jump.**

ammunition containers, radios, smoke grenades, and camouflage netting, and have ranges in excess of 498 miles (800 km).

Another wheeled vehicle that has enjoyed great success with the American military is the High Mobility Multi-Purpose Wheeled Vehicle (HMMWV), or "Hummer." The vehicle's light aluminum body makes it ideal for transportation in the fuselage of a transport aircraft or slung underneath a helicopter—two can be carried by a Chinook, one by a Black Hawk, and up to 15 in the fuselage of a C-5 Galaxy aircraft.

The revolutionary dune-buggy type vehicle employed by American and British special forces has a number of advantages over larger vehicles such as the Jeep and Land Rover. It is easier to conceal and to transport by air, it is more nimble, and it presents

**This HMMWV patrol vehicle is armed with a MK 19 automatic grenade launcher. With a maximum speed of around 77 miles per hour (128 km/h), it can attack enemy positions quickly.**

a smaller target to the enemy. Models such as the Chenworth Fast Attack Vehicle (FAV), the Wessex Saker, and Longline's Light Strike Vehicle (LSV) have powerful engines and can mount a variety of weapons, including machine guns, canons, and anti-tank missiles. Such vehicles were used to great effect in the Gulf War by SAS and SEAL teams to hit targets behind Iraqi lines.

Insertion onto an enemy coastline has long been practiced by elite forces, from small teams of the British Special Boat Squadron (SBS) and American SEALs, to full-scale invasions such as at D-Day and Iwo Jima in World War II. The U.S. Navy currently operates some 65 amphibious vessels. Some of these can be very big indeed. One type can carry 1,700 troops, four Harrier fighter aircraft, two CH-46 Sea Knight helicopters, 10 CH-53 helicopters, and one UH-1N helicopter.

Both the United States and Russia also employ numerous hovercraft and landing craft air cushion (LCAC) vessels. The latter are able to carry a variety of cargo, including main battle tanks, and can reach high speeds. These craft have a number of advantages over traditional ships. They have high speeds, the

**The Chinook helicopter can lift 7,262 pounds (3,294 kg) of weight and transport it over 200 miles (320 km) before landing it when needed.**

ability to travel over water and flat land, and they can carry a lot of equipment. Other smaller vessels used by special forces include the two-person Klepper canoe deployed by the SBS and various inflatable commando craft. One of these is the sub-skimmer made by Submarine Products Ltd. Sixteen feet (5 m) long and capable of a surface speed of 27 **knots**, this craft can convert to a mini-submarine and carry up to four divers.

Elite units have earned their fame in battle by the careful selection of the soldier, weapons and equipment, and the unit's tactics. Training and combat bring these various elements into an effective fighting force. Highly specialized roles, such as participation in covert (secret) operations, require an even higher degree of selection and training. Competitions and exercises, held by units such as the Royal Marines and British Parachute Regiment, put great emphasis on effective shooting after completing long, exhausting endurance marches.

Surprise and speed are essential to the commando and airborne roles, and night shooting is vital for such units as the British Special Air Service and Navy SEALs. Foreign weapons training is an essential skill in Special Force's "A-Teams." Because they operate so far from base, it is likely that special forces soldiers will run out of ammunition for their own weapons and have to use the enemy's. In the closing stages of the Arnhem battle during World War II, for example, isolated areas of the airborne perimeter were held only because British paratroops fought with captured weapons and ammunition. Firearms training is particularly intense for counterterrorist units. In an average year, a German

**Inflatable boats can be deflated and hidden easily on landing. However, they can be easily sunk by enemy bullets.**

**The Rigid Raider assault boat is used by many elite forces. It can carry up to eight people and has a 140 horsepower outboard motor.**

## U.S. NAVY SEALs UNDERWATER EQUIPMENT

The U.S. Navy SEALs have an amazing variety of equipment to perform their underwater missions. When they are on diving operations, they use special breathing apparatus that does not release clouds of bubbles when the wearer breathes out. This is important, as it stops sentries on ships or on shore spotting clouds of bubbles that tell him there is a diver below. However, the SEALs have methods of getting to their targets. They also use what are called Special Delivery Vehicles. These are like miniature submarines. The SEAL diver sits in one and drives it underwater to his target. Once there, the diver can stick explosive charges to the bottom of a boat, or abandon the craft and head inshore. These are just two of the items that help the SEALs do their job expertly. Other equipment used by the SEALs include: the seven-person inflatable boat, handheld sonar and underwater communication devices, and various types of parachute for land and water jumps.

counterterrorist unit member fires more than 8,000 rounds during training!

However, marksmanship and good equipment in themselves do not win battles or rescue hostages; self-discipline and teamwork are also important. Many elite unit actions are won by personal courage and standards, not just the tools of war.

# GLOSSARY

**Abseiled** Descended quickly down a cliff face or building using a rope wrapped around the body.

**Allies** In World War II, the Allies were those countries who fought against Germany and Japan.

**American Civil War** A war between the Northern and Southern states of the United States, which lasted from 1861–1865.

**American Revolutionary War** A five-year war (1775–1783), in which the people of the United States overthrew British rule.

**Colony** A country that is ruled by another country. For example, for a long time India was a British colony.

**Commonwealth** In Britain, the Commonwealth refers to a group of countries that used to be British colonies, but which now cooperate together as friendly nations.

**Communism** A political idea which states that the government owns all property and gives to the people according to their needs.

**Confederacy** The 11 Southern states of the United States that fought against the Northern states in the Civil War.

**D-Day** Refers to June 6, 1944 when a massive Allied force invaded France and began the liberation of Europe from the Germans.

**Dinghy** An inflatable life raft made of rubber.

**DZ** Stands for "Drop Zone," the place where airborne soldiers land on an operation.

**Falklands War** A war in 1982 that resulted after Argentina invaded and occupied the British Falkland Islands. The British sent a huge military force and took the islands back.

**Freefall** A technique of parachuting, in which the parachutist falls long distances without opening his parachute.

**Grenada** An island in the Caribbean, which was invaded by the United States after the government was overthrown there in 1983.

**Guerrilla** A guerrilla soldier does not belong to a regular army and generally fights using tactics of ambush and terrorism.

**Gulf War** A war that happened in 1991 after Iraq invaded the small neighboring country of Kuwait. The United States led a massive international army, which eventually defeated Iraq and pushed its soldiers back out of Kuwait.

**Holocaust** The Holocaust refers to the terrible period of human history during World War II, in which six million Jews were killed on orders from the German government.

**Knots** A measurement of speed equal to one nautical mile (6,076 feet/ 1,852 m) per hour.

**Korean War** A war between North and South Korea (1950–53), which became an international conflict with the United States and many other nations involved.

**Palestine** An ancient territory in the Middle East, which is now Israel. However, many Arabs still call it Palestine and treat Israel as an occupier.

**RAAF** Stands for the Royal Australian Air Force.

**Reconnaissance** The military term for exploring and gathering information about the enemy and terrain, often done secretly.

**Russian Revolution** A revolution in Russia that occurred in 1917. The old government of the Tzar was overthrown and a new communist government under Lenin was established.

**Sabre Squadron** The name given to each of the four combat squadrons of the SAS.

**Soviet Union** A massive group of 15 countries, which existed as one single country ruled under communism. It lasted until 1991.

**Sultan** A head of government of a Muslim state.

**Viet Cong** The name given to the Vietnamese communists who fought a guerrilla war in South Vietnam during the Vietnam War.

**Vietnam War** A war between South and North Vietnam, which lasted from the early 1960s to 1975. The U.S. was involved in the war for over 10 years.

**Winston Churchill** The British Prime Minister during World War II, famous for his defiance of the Germans.

# RECRUITMENT INFORMATION

**The British Army (SAS)**

To enter the Special Air Service, you have to be a serving soldier in the British Army of Commonwealth forces. (Sometimes other foreign nationals are considered; always check first.) You have to have a good record of soldiering and also have about three years of military service remaining.

Selection for the SAS is very tough. Courses are run twice a year, in the summer and winter. Few people make it through—of every 150 people who start the selection course, only about 15 people actually pass, sometimes fewer. For those who are considering entering the SAS, a career in the British Army is the first step. For more information on the SAS, go to the following websites:

http://www.army.mod.uk

http://www.specwarnet.com/europe/sas.htm

http://www.geocities.com/alli_cool_dood/

**The U.S. Army**

The U.S. Army is a massive organization and offers a wide range of careers. These include positions like cooks and bandsmen, to elite combat roles such as the Special Forces and Airborne Forces. U.S. Army recruiting offices can be found throughout the United States and also abroad.

However, if you are interested in finding out more about the U.S. Army and U.S. Airborne Forces check out the following websites:

http://www.usarmy.com

http://members.aol.com/army/sof1/ASOC.html

http://www.ammil.com/p0000187.htm

http://www.screamingeagles.org

http://members.tripod.com/thede/airborne.html

http://members.aol.com/demojumper

**Australian Army**

Entry into the Australian SAS is every bit as tough as its British equivalent. Like the British SAS, you need to be a regular soldier first. To join the Australian Army, you need to be an Australian citizen between 17 and 35 years of age. You have to go through a series of interviews and medical and intelligence tests before being assigned to an appropriate selection course. You will also have to do a fitness test. Like the other armies described here, there are many types of job in the Australian Army.

For information on the Australian Army check out the the following websites:

http://www.army.gov.au
http://www.armyjobs.defence.gov.au
http://www.101.net.au
http://www.omen.net.au/eaglem/rae
http://iol.com.au/conway/ww1/army.html

# ELITE UNITS OF THE WORLD

*Unit:* GSG-9
*Country:* Germany
*Year formed:* 1972
*Example of operations:* Rescuing 87 hostages from a hijacked airliner at Mogadishu, Somalia, 1977

*Unit:* Gurkhas
*Country:* United Kingdom
*Year formed:* 1815
*Example of operations:* Took part in some of the final battles of the Falklands War to liberate the capital, Port Stanley.

*Unit:* The Parachute Regiment
*Country:* United Kingdom
*Year formed:* 1940
*Example of operations:* The courageous, but disastrous, mission to capture a bridge at Arnhem from the Germans in 1944, during World War II.

*Unit:* Special Air Service
*Country:* United Kingdom
*Year formed:* 1942
*Example of operations:* Rescuing hostages from the Iranian Embassy in London in 1980.

*Unit:* U.S. Army Special
Operations Forces
*Country:* United States
*Year formed:* 1952
*Example of operations:* Fighting
communist guerrillas in the
jungle during the Vietnam War.

*Unit:* U.S. Army Rangers
*Country:* United States
*Year formed:* 1942
*Example of operations:* Scaled
cliffs to attack German positions
during the Allied invasion of
German-occupied Europe in
1944.

*Unit:* 82nd Airborne Division
*Country:* United States
*Year formed:* 1940s
*Example of operations:* Some of
the leading troops taking part in
the attack against Iraqi forces
during the Gulf War.

*Unit:* U.S. Marine Corps
*Country:* United States
*Year formed:* 1775
*Example of operations:* Led U.S.
forces in recapturing Japanese-
held islands in the Pacific
during WWII.

*Unit:* U.S. Navy SEALS
*Country:* United States
*Year formed:* 1962
*Example of operations:* Rescuing U.S.
prisoners of war in the Vietnam War.

*Unit:* Spetsnaz
*Country:* Russia
*Year formed:* 1950s
*Example of operations:* Attacking
guerrilla strongholds in the
mountains of Afghanistan during the
1980s.

*Unit:* Australian Special Air Service
*Country:* Australia
*Year formed:* 1957
*Example of operations:* Fighting
against the Viet Cong communists.

*Unit:* Israeli Special Forces
*Country:* Israel
*Year formed:* 1948
*Example of operations:* Assassinating
Arab guerrilla and military leaders
during the many wars between Israel
and Arab nations.